# MODERN ACROSTICS FOR YOUNGER READERS

**Ken Waldman**

# MODERN ACROSTICS FOR YOUNGER READERS

**Ken Waldman**

Ridgeway Press
Roseville, Michigan

Copyright©2025 Ken Waldman
ISBN: 978-1-56439-087-5

**Ridgeway Press**
P.O. Box 120, Roseville MI 48066

No part of this book may be reproduced or transmitted in any form or by any means electronic, mechanical, photocopying, or otherwise, without the express written consent of Ken Waldman.

**Acknowledgments:**

This was the culmination of many years of writing and travel. Thanks to the many who invited me to their communities and schools. Without those invitations, I wouldn't/couldn't have written the poems here.

While I've privately circulated some of these acrostic poems over the years, a few found their way in journals. Those are listed below. I thank those editors at *Poets & Writers Magazine*.

Also, a big thanks to M.L. Liebler of Ridgeway Press whose support has been crucial.

A few friends and colleagues I especially have to thank by name: Alex Carollo (all those Slidell and Slidell school poems!), Richard Haerther, David Palmer, Shane Cadman, Jaclyn Wood, Heidi Sheridan, Sarah Jo Lightner, Nick Littman, Jack Rogers, Dulcie Willis, Alan Liddell, Michael Burgraff, Johanna Kodlick. Apologies to everybody else who helped along the way and whose names I've omitted here — there are lots of you (and you're all amazing)!

*Poets & Writers Magazine:* "Bellamy" "Bellamy$^2$"

# Table of Contents

## I
Aliso Viejo + Soka ........................................................................ 2
Temecula ........................................................................................ 3
Lancaster + Palmdale² ................................................................. 4
Broadoaks + Broadoaks² + Whittier² ......................................... 5
Butte County + Neal Dow ............................................................ 6
Carlsbad² ........................................................................................ 7
Louisiana + Abney² ....................................................................... 8
Slidell + Slidell + Slidell² + Slidell² ............................................ 9
Brock Elementary + Brock Elementary + Brock² ..................... 10
Dolby Elementary School ............................................................ 12
Carencro and Lafayette ................................................................ 13
Bayou Woods + Bayou Woods .................................................... 14
Whispering Forest + Whispering Forest .................................... 15
Little Oak + Little Oak² ................................................................ 16
St. Tammany Parish + St. Tammany Parish² ............................. 17
Author's Tea + Author's Tea² ...................................................... 18

## II
Lake Jackson ................................................................................. 20
Bellamy + Bellamy² ...................................................................... 21
Pahrump + Blanding² ................................................................... 22
Blaisdell Elementary + Blaisdell² ............................................... 23
School Street Elementary + School Street² ............................... 24
Tuscarawas .................................................................................... 26
Montessori + Montessori² ............................................................ 27
Bellefontaine Intermediate School + Logan County² ............... 28
Austin Tracy Elementary ............................................................. 30
LeGrande² + James E. Bazzell .................................................... 31
Moab Charter School ................................................................... 32
Ophir Elementary ......................................................................... 33
Fred A. Anderson + Oriental + Pamlico² ................................... 34
Helen Hyatt Elementary .............................................................. 35
Laurel Elementary + Tavelli Elementary .................................. 36
Shepardson STEM Elementary + Lincoln Center² ................... 38

## III
Grant County + Grant County² ................................................... 41
Fergus Falls ................................................................................... 42
Otter Tail County + Otter Tail County² ..................................... 43

Bigfork, Minnesota + Itasca County .......................................... 44
Trapper Creek Elementary .......................................... 45
Talkeetna Elementary .......................................... 46
Kelly Elementary + Lewisburg .......................................... 47
Linntown Intermediate .......................................... 48
Seabury School[2] .......................................... 49
Clinton Public + Clinton Public[2] .......................................... 50
Denti[2] + Gansevoort .......................................... 51

## IV

Monroe Central[2] .......................................... 53
Bloomington .......................................... 54
Caston[2] + Caston[2] .......................................... 55
Thompson[2] + OJ Neighbours[2] .......................................... 56
Lincoln + Lincoln[2] .......................................... 57
Manchester Intermediate[2] .......................................... 58
Ocean County + Ocean County[2] .......................................... 59
Silver Bay Elementary .......................................... 60
Bayville Elementary .......................................... 61
Ocean Gate Elementary .......................................... 62
Syracuse[2] + Fifth Street .......................................... 63
Transitions .......................................... 64

## V

Methow Valley Elementary .......................................... 66
East Omak Elementary .......................................... 67
Sammamish + Sammamish .......................................... 68
Green Hill + Northeast .......................................... 69
Cochise County + Cochise County[2] .......................................... 70
Enterprise Elementary School .......................................... 71
Seven Locks[2] .......................................... 72
Houston Clear Lake .......................................... 73
Athens Autumn Harvest Moon Fest + Woodford[2] .......................................... 74
St. Paul Elementary .......................................... 76
Littleton Academy .......................................... 77
Allen County[2] + Allen County Intermediate .......................................... 78
Illuminations .......................................... 80
Alton[2] .......................................... 81

**Coda**
My Poem is Here .......................................... 83

*for Hal & Lisa, for Melissa, for Lenny & Rachel,*

*and most of all for Ava Jade and Este*

This collection is the direct result of a crowdfunding campaign. Every one of these backers helped make this print edition a reality: Paul Fericano, Rachael Fulbright & Charlie Carew, Elizabeth English, Hal & Lisa Tovin, Mark Tamsula, Barbara Rosner, Suzanne Todd, Stephanie Dickie, David Epley, Jennifer Spector, Sidney Myer, Alexis Knudsen, Jim Kruger, Sallie Mack & Jonathan Freese, Llysa Holland, Emily Pinkerton, Jamie Hascall, Jordan Wankoff, Jerry Hagins, Beth Chrisman, Eric Graves, Rich Russell, Cheryl Chrisman, Caitlin Warbelow, David McCormick, Maureen Kelly, Ellen Ferguson, Claire Holland LeClair, John Carnahan, Jay Best, Anne-Marie Holen, Susan Martin, Beth Nelson, Gabriel Furtado, Jeff Yeckel, Storm Walker, Perry Haaland, Hugh Robertson, Juan Romano, Bernard Ussher, Robert Daniel, David Volk, Jim Clark, Jeff Talmadge, Alison Moore, David Palmer, Emily Bunning, Joshua Kane, Chad Herzog, Jeff Corle, Kayla Oelhafen, Robert Baird, Tia Regan, Beth Nelson, Scott Sparling, John Freeman Jr., Michael Alexander, John Bunch, Stephanie Smith-Leckness, Hiren Amin. I deeply thank them!

# I

## Aliso Viejo + Soka

Any time you see a poem,
look both ways, almost as
if you're crossing a street.
Slow down. Read the words
one by one. You might find

very serious things, sad things,
important things, silly things,
extra-special things, strange things.
Just read and reread words
one by one. Then read another poem.

+

Some days are blue
or orange. Some days are
kind of like purple. Reading
a good book, you're in a rainbow.

**Temecula**

There are towns where
everyone is lucky to be near
mountain, lake, and ocean,
enjoying sunny days with friends.
Can you think of such places?
Up in Alaska there are only a few.
Lots more here in California —
and it's also much warmer

## Lancaster + Palmdale[2]

Lots to write about
all the time. You might
notice the sky, big
clouds forming. You might see
a dead animal, or else
smell a skunk. You might pretend
to be a dinosaur or shark.
Everyone has amazing ideas. By
reading others, you learn your own.

+

Please remember I'm tricky. I make up
a lot of poems. Some about California.
Lots about different favorite foods. I'll
mention pizza. Then there's ice cream.
Doughnuts, anyone? And who would
appreciate a taco or burrito or even a
large milkshake? Yes, I can spend all
evening eating. Then time to exercise.

## Broadoaks + Broadoaks² + Whittier²

Be a reader. That means
reading all the time. Read
on weekends alone. Read
at a friend's house upside-down. Read
despite feeling hungry, tired, sick.
One day, if you read enough,
a funny thing happens. You'll
keep dreaming in words. You'll
sleep inside sentences, wake with stories.

+

Best to wait in line. Do not push or grab.
Recess begins by marching out the door
one by one right when it's the time to go
and play. Here's another very good idea.
Don't hit. Don't shout. Don't be too loud
or mean. Be polite. You can always try to
ask friends to be quiet and to then share a
king-sized peanut, or grape, or sip of milk.
Silly! This poem is silly. I'm quite serious.

+

Watch me do something new.
How is this different? I rush
into the air. Yes, like a bird I
take off and swoop with fast
talky flapping, taking flight
in images. Friend, it's like I
exist to soar through space.
Remember this, dear reader.

**Butte County + Neal Dow**

Best to be honest. Better not
use your mom or dad's favorite
things unless you get permission.
This is very important: make
every day the best day ever.

Can I tell you how poems are
one of the most amazing things.
Use poems to tell stories. You can
name things in poems: sky, mountain,
thunder, wind, rain, star, moon.
You can include your dog.

+

Nothing much is better than two or three
electric guitars for certain songs. Who prefers
a piano, or a wooden flute? Who prefers
loud brass horns, or a solo violin? Who'd like to play

drums? How about a harmonica? I really can go
on and on about music. There's so much to hear.
What's your favorite instrument? Do you like to sing?

## Carlsbad[2]

Choose a lively time full of music
and stories, even a trip to Alaska.
Reach a goal, then reach farther,
letting yourself swim, fly, or sail.
Sometimes the wind will say yes,
being your best friend. Take a stab
at making art (maybe art is an idea
describing big rock or tree or cloud).

## Louisiana + Abney[2]

Let yourself think
of great adventure
up in your minds.
Imagination is a most
special friend. With
imagination you can own
any idea, any time, anywhere.
Never will you be bored.
A whole world awaits.

+

Ask me a question about Alaska.
Be curious. Yes, we do have crab.
No snakes. But owl, bear, salmon.
Everyone in Alaska knows moose.
You must come and visit some day.

## Slidell + Slidell + Slidell² + Slidell²

Some poems might be about
love. Some might have parades.
I write those and more. Cats,
dogs, a slice of pizza. Poems about
eating, about reading, about running
late, or running fast. I write
lots of poems. You can too.

+

Silly, who is ever silly?
Let me ask you next
if you've ever been serious.
Don't even think about it. Yes,
everyone has been silly and serious.
Lucky you're silly and serious boys and girls
living in a warm and wonderful place.

+

Such a warm, friendly town. Kids
laugh and tell good jokes. They'll
invite you over. They might say hi.
Don't worry if you don't get invited.
Everyone I know has some of those
long and unhappy times. Here, I'll
let you hear my big secret. Be cool!

+

Some weeks it really rains
like the sky is broken. All
it takes is one dark cloud. I
don't like when it rains hard.
Everyone has to stay inside.
Little kids can't run and yell.
Let's hope today is beautiful.

## Brock Elementary + Brock Elementary + Brock²

Books can take you everywhere.
Read one and you might go to
Oklahoma. Read another and you're in
Colorado or California, or maybe on some
kind of rocket or inside a submarine.

Every book can teach you. Some make you
laugh or cry. Some show you how to cook
eggs or bake cookies or cakes. Some may
make you want to go far away to
explore mountains, oceans, or outer space. Some may
not have any words at all—just beautiful pictures.
The library is the most amazing place because
anyone can go and take books home to
read. Once you read, you can go anywhere.
You don't even have to pay!

+

Be an amazing beaver—
really, beavers are my favorites
of all animals. Some people prefer
cheetahs or whales or wolves or
kangaroos. Some people prefer

elephants or camels or
little bitty kitty cats or maybe
eagles or dolphins or bears or
moose (and in Alaska
everybody gives moose lots of space—
no one ever wants
to tangle with them).
A few people really like
rabbits or squirrels or gophers. I ask
you: what's your favorite?

+

Bonus points if you've sat in a bathtub reading a favorite book. Yes, that is far out. You can read anywhere. You can go camping and read (and even read music). Know that you can even read in the dark.

**Dolby Elementary School**

Don't run in the halls
or be a bully. Don't
litter anywhere. Don't do
beastly things to any of
your family or friends. Don't

eat mosquitoes. Don't
lose your shoes. Don't
ever swallow stones. Don't
make trouble at recess. Don't
embarrass your mom. Don't
nag your teacher. Don't
touch a hot plate. Don't climb
a dead tree. Don't don't don't
race to the bathroom. Don't say
*yes* when you mean *no*. Don't

say *no* when you mean *yes*. Don't cry
crocodile tears. Don't try to hide
hamsters in underwear. But do read this poem
over and over. And do learn
one new thing every single day. And, yes, do
love the Earth, and your fellow classmates.

## Carencro and Lafayette

Choose your superheroes
and make a plan.
Read about them
everyday. Become them.
Next you'll find you
can climb higher, or fly.
Read about superheroes everyday.
Once you read, you can soar.

And once you start soaring,
no one can ever stop you.
Do you want to be a superhero?

Let me tell you how
a superhero is born.
First, they discover
a special talent.
You all have one,
every one of you.
The trick is to use it,
then keep using it.
Everyone can be a superhero.

## Bayou Woods² + Bayou Woods²

By now you know your job
at school. Here in Louisiana
you know heat, football, joy.
Of course you read books to
understand new things. If you

want to know math or know
old stories, open a book. Go
open one—you may learn to
dance, or fly. We've all read
so many books over the years.


+


Books can take you off any old curb
and fly you from Louisiana to Iowa.
You might go to Utah or Kentucky.
Or else to Oklahoma or Colorado.
Up you go. And it's all from you

welcoming in books. This is how.
Open yourself to Oregon or Ohio
or Pennsylvania. You might go to
Delaware. Books make you glad.
So read more about our 50 states.

## Whispering Forest + Whispering Forest

What's the best color? Is it red, blue, yellow?
How about orange, green, pink? Many people
in Louisiana think it's purple. Who here can
say their favorite animals? Are they horses, cows,
pigs? What about dogs, cats, snakes? What about
eagles? What about whales? Who here loves to
run? Who here loves to read? Who here loves to go
in the library and take home books for free? Who here
never has been to Florida? Who here likes
going to New Orleans? Who here likes

foggy days? Who here likes the wind, the rain,
or the cold? What makes some children
run so fast? Who here really loves to
eat dessert? Who loves apples? Who
sometimes eats popcorn or hot dogs or
tacos? Who here is tired of questions?

+

When you read a book,             ,
here's what you want to remember.
If the book is exciting, don't
stop, and keep turning those
pages. It's like you're inside this
exciting dream. As you continue
reading, it's almost like you're also
in the book and are your own exciting
new character there. Keep
going. All those other characters are new

friends. And as the reader, you're now
one of them. As you
read, you can now imagine how
every story is an adventurous ride.
So be brave, my creature friends. By reading
these words, you've now gone inside a poem.

Ken Waldman / 15

**Little Oak + Little Oak²**

Lots to write about all the time.
I can write about mom or dad,
toothaches or pancakes, glue or rock,
twenty-two wishes or a bar of soap.
Lots to write about all the time.
Everyone has that talent.

One thing you might write
about is what you notice right now.
Keep looking. Write what you see.

+

Let me tell you my secret. All
I can say is keep alert. Yes, I
try to notice things. Be alert!
That's it, the great big secret.
Let me share an extra-special
extraordinary secret right here

on paper. Poems can take you to
another realm, as bubbly as cola,
kind as grandma. Find a fun book.

### St. Tammany Parish + St. Tammany Parish[2]

Sometimes we're excited. Sometimes,
tired. Sometimes the only thing we want

to do is order a big burrito,
and then ice cream for dessert.
Maybe you're hungry right now.
Maybe you're happy. Maybe, sad.
Anything is possible because
no two days are alike.
You and I do the best we can,

promising to do even better tomorrow.
An idea for you. How about
reading about rare wild animals
in Africa. Or a mountain adventure in
South America. Or a ghost story
here and now. What's exciting?

+

Short ones, tall ones. Some with glasses
to see the world. Some love making art,

trying to make shape and color perfect.
Artists are amazing. They take an idea
most people won't notice, as if a dream.
Messy ones, neat ones. Some are from
a bigger town, some from a small area.
Nothing is impossible. But please listen.
You can never be anybody else. No way.

Proud ones, loud ones. Some who'll keep
a promise, some who will eat your pizza.
Rich ones, poor ones, some who travel far—
India, Japan, Canada, Spain, even Hawaii.
Some go to Baton Rouge or New Orleans.
How to create a special life? Make a wish.

## Author's Tea + Author's Tea[2]

Any book can teach you how to better
understand the world you live. It can
teach you how to care for a puppy, or
how to howl like a wolf. Books can
offer you good information about
rabbits, kittens, horses, skunks,
squirrels, eagles, butterflies, and more.

That's why we love libraries so much.
Everything in the world can be found there,
and that means books you might some day write.

+

A tall man from faraway Alaska
uses a pen and blank paper. You
too can make the best books. It
has to be fun for you. So much
of writing can transport you to
real adventures. Yes, every year
so very many great new stories

to read. Keep reading. Don't quit.
Every day you can go anywhere:
Argentina, Australia, even Africa.

# II

**Lake Jackson**

Little kids and big kids
are here today. Some
kids read a lot
every single day. Some kids

just read a little bit.
All kids are different.
Can you show me which
kids here love to read? Can you
show me which kids love to swim?
One thing I wonder: Who has
no fear—who is strong and brave?

## Bellamy + Bellamy[2]

Boys and girls sit in
every class. Some
love reading. Some love
lunch. Some love
art and music. Some love
math. Some love poems.
You, what do you love?

+

Be a bobcat. Don't be a crab.
Eat a great big juicy orange,
lots of vegetables too. We'll
look out the windows. Will
an animal walk by? Florida
makes me happy. Yes, I'm
your poetry friend today.
.

## Pahrump + Blanding[2]

Please tell me if you have
a favorite animal. Some kids love
horses. Others love dogs or cats.
Rabbits can be lots of fun
unless you have to catch one.
Monkey see. Monkey do.
Please don't play with a porcupine.

+


Before you step off the curb,
look both ways. Is that all?
Also pay attention. An idea
needs to be written down
Don't forget to have a pad
in your pocket to write. I
never forget to carry a pen.
Good ideas deserve writing.

## Blaisdell Elementary + Blaisdell[2]

Be good. Yes, be good.
Love your mom and dad
and the cereal you eat
in the morning. Love
small puppy dogs. Love
dirt and grass and trees.
Everything can be loved.
Love books and school.
Love your teachers. Love

each day. Love
large things like
elephants. Love
music—it can be
easy to learn. Yes,
never stop loving
the world. Love
a flower. Love
rivers. Love reading.
Yes, love the library

+

Burp the baby. Babies grab
lots of things. They're small
and sleepy. In Pennsylvania
I see so many little babies. I
say some of you see babies
drinking milk or eating food.
Each baby can be so very cute.
Little babies might really smell.
Let them some day be very tall.

## School Street Elementary + School Street[2]

Sometimes poems
can be silly, smart,
happy, or sad.
Or else mean.
Or else loving.
Lots of poems

seem to
tell a story.
Read this closely,
eyes on the words.
Each of you may
take it differently.

Each of you
learns differently.
Each of you
may see different things.
Each of you may
notice something
that the others won't.
A poem can
really show
you the world.

+

Start reading this and open your minds.
Choose to see music here. Or the magic.
How about seeing a great big bike crash.
Or a little bitty stomach ache. Yes? No?
One other thing a poem might do is to
let you imagine a brand new basketball

swishing through a net. Or else hot dogs, tacos, pizza, ice cream, a really big feast. Right now, a poem might have a teacher explaining a problem, or it might include eagles, hawks, especially owls. This one teaches you to see and feel quite brilliant.

**Tuscarawas**

Time to read a poem that takes you
up to the brain and down below
small feet and toes. I know you
can read this poem, which is
also about happiness, sadness, lunch,
recess, even the library. It's even
about reading, math, and questions.
Who loves libraries? Who loves puzzles?
Are you happy today? Are you sad?
Something I want to know: Was lunch good?

## Montessori + Montessori²

Many kids love to
own a pet. I wonder
now if any of you have
turtles, or goldfish, or
even an eel. Who has a dog?
Someone have a kitten?
Someone have a snake
or a parrot? You can
read about all animals by going
into a library.

+

Maybe you like turkey, ham,
or green salad. Or you like to
nibble on a blueberry muffin.
There are always things to eat,
eat, eat. Who likes some cheese?
Some of you like oranges. Yes?
Some of you like burritos. Yes?
Or would you rather have a taco—
rice, beans, and a whole dinner?
Ice cream is fun. So is spaghetti.

## Bellefontaine Intermediate School + Logan County[2]

Beware of people who think they know
everything. We all know
lots and lots. You and I know
little things, big things, hard things,
easy things. But none of us know every
fantastic or foolish thing. Some of us know about
old dogs or cats. Some of us know about
new puppies or kittens. Some of us know about
tasty tacos or burritos. Some of us know
about tasty chocolate chips
inside cookies. Some of us think we know
nothing (but that's not true—we all know things).
Everything? No one knows everything.

If you like to read books, you'll
never stop learning exciting new
things. You can learn about China
Egypt, Brazil. You can learn about
rhinos, hippos, polar bears. You can
maybe learn about hawks, vultures, ravens
eagles. You can learn about love,
death, adventure. You can learn about
Indians (and even Chieftains). You can learn
about oceans, outer space, robots. You can learn about
tigers, horses, snakes. But you can't learn
everything—everything is too big.

Smart people know that they absolutely
can't know everything. But they're
happy to keep learning. They'll read about
owls, otters, ostriches, lots of
other creatures. They'll read about
llamas, leopards, ladybugs, lions.

+

Let's make something extra-special.
Open your big & beautiful minds to
go learn about climbing or traveling.
A mountain summit. A trip to Alaska.
Never say never. Instead think when.

Choose to do something new. Music
or another activity. Who wants to go
up in a blue hot air balloon? Do you?
No, I'm not kidding. The world is fun.
The world is big, wild, and abundant.
Yes, you're living in this world today.

**Austin Tracy Elementary**

A poem can take you
up a mountain, or can
slide you to the ground.
There are poems that put you
inside a dog's brain.
No, I'm not kidding. Woof!

This poem teaches you that
reading poems can be fun.
A poem can also have
cats meowing. Meow. Meow.
Yes, poems can have eagles, eels,

elephants, one or two unicorns.
Lions, too. Tigers, too. A seal.
Even dinosaurs. A poem
might have horses, pigs,
even reindeer, even wolves.
Never think you know it all.
That's one more thing
about poems. You can
read them and learn something
you never knew before.

## LeGrande[2] + James E. Bazzell

Little second-graders walk down a hall
each morning carrying an orange, apple,
grapes, or a banana. Or maybe carrying
really yummy chocolate chip cookies, or
a candy bar. Or even a big slice of pizza.
No one should go hungry. It's great fun
deciding what to eat next. Hard-boiled
eggs are always good. So is a popsicle.

+

Just let me have
a minute of your time. Or
maybe five minutes. Or
even ten minutes. I have
something to explain to

each of you. Don't

be nervous when reading or writing poems.
A poem can do almost anything. They can
zip quick down a page. They can
zap your brain. Zip here. Zap there. They'll
even zoom through and show you
love, death, Kentucky, Alaska,
life on a farm, life in a city, life as a dream.

## Moab Charter School

Must be the week
of poetry, music,
art. It's about
best friends

creating what's
happy, funny, sad. It's
about colors —
reds, greens, blues.
There's a violin
every morning.
Real music — simple

sounds and songs.
Can we write poems?
How can we not? Write
one word. Another.
Open up to fun,
laughter, inspiration, surprise.

## Ophir Elementary

One thing I must tell you, my friends.
Please listen closely. I'll say now
how every single word
in the world can be yours.
Rivers, mountains, valleys,

even the big skies you
love so much here. Sun, moon,
even stars can be yours.
Moms, dads, sisters, brothers,
especially your dogs or cats.
New shoes or old shirts can be yours.
Toys, too. So can hamburgers
and hot dogs. So can green, orange,
red, and yellow leaves. Pumpkins, too.
Your wishes and dreams can be yours.

## Fred A. Anderson + Oriental + Pamlico[2]

Friends are everywhere if you
really want to make them. How
easy is it to make a new friend?
Do this: Listen to someone's story

and ask a few questions.

A good listener can be a friend.
No, don't interrupt. What else?
Do this. Always be truthful. And be
eager to be helpful when you
realize someone needs help.
Send good wishes. You all can
only be yourselves. Every day gives you
new chances to become a friend.

+

One thing you all can
read here is the water.
If you don't, you'll learn.
Every week brings its changes.
Nights and days continue.
The river has a rhythm
and its role. If you
live here, you have yours.

+

Please and thank you. Do not drop
a plate and break it. Here's an idea:
make a gift for your dad or mom.
Let it be something that will still
interest them for a whole year. I
can't tell you what that is. Music
or artwork is very amazing to do.

## Helen Hyatt Elementary

Hello. How are you?
Everyone healthy today?
Let me add together
everything you know:
new toys, old clothes,

happy and sad memories,
your favorite ice cream,
a pet dog or cat, a game.
This list even includes
the school you attend. Yes,

everything you know is here:
laughing, crying, sleeping,
eating, reading, recess,
math, science, history,
Earth, Mars, Jupiter,
nice people, mean people,
tall people, tiny people,
a best friend, a second best friend,
rain, snow, sunshine, wind,
you, your family, your dreams.

## Laurel Elementary + Tavelli Elementary

Let me tell you a little secret.
Anyone can play violin. All of
us are lucky since all we
really need is an instrument. Play
every day, even if only for a minute.
Let me tell you another secret.

Everyone has a talent. Some
love to do math. Some love to run far.
Everyone is different. Some love
music so much they'll play
every day for an hour or more.
No two people are the same
(though twins can be very much alike).
Anyone can play violin. I was
rather old when I started.
You're all very lucky to play here.

+

Tell me a story. Maybe it's
about your summer
vacation. Think back. What was
extra fun? Did you visit places?
Lakes, maybe? A library? Who here
loves reading new books?
If so, please raise your hand.

Every day there are
lots of things to do.
Eat, play, read, sleep.
Most every day we're
eager for adventure.
Never stop learning.
That's why we get up
and get dressed.
Read and reread these words.
Yes, begin telling your own story!

## Shepardson STEM Elementary + Lincoln Center[2]

Sometimes I like to show
how everything in the world can
exist in your imagination.
Penguins? Think about them. Or else
a picture of some trees,
rocks, and dirt. How about
dancing, jumping, and playing at recess.
Some of you may imagine flying far
over the moon. Some of you are
noisy and some are quiet.

Some of you like to visit
Texas. Others like to
eat pizza or tacos, or drink
milk while eating pie.

Everything can be in your imagination.
Light and dark. Polka dots and stripes—
every color in the rainbow.
Men, women, and children. Dogs, too,
especially friendly ones. Yes,
no, maybe. Stars, too. Yesterday,
today, and tomorrow. Think how
a dream can be inside a dream.
Right, left, forwards, backwards.
You never know what's next.

+

Listen closely as I show and tell
in front of you all. Here's what I
need to say. Books are really fun.
Come see how it's just like magic.
Open a book. It might take you to
live on a mountain. Maybe it will
nag you to take a bath to get clean.

Come read. Books are like magic.
Earth is big. You might dig inside
near the middle. Or find the moon.
There's a wonderful world to meet.
Enter a book. It can be a dream. Be
ready for stories. Be the best reader.

III

## Grant County + Grant County²

Great things can happen when you
read something that excites you.
A book can sweep you into
nature—volcanoes, coral reefs,
thunderstorms. Libraries let you

choose whatever you want to see, hear,
or learn. You can read about galaxies
up in space. Or study how birds make
nests. Or you can see movies. Or listen
to symphonies. Maybe you'll learn to build
your own robot. Nothing is impossible.

+

Get in the choir if you like to sing.
Run fast in a race—then run faster
and faster. Come with a good idea.
No whining is allowed—have fun
today and tonight for tomorrow it

can rain. People here listen to music
on radio or YouTube. That's how to
use science now. We hope that you
next start on an instrument. Go on.
Try and learn. It's not too difficult.
You can play the drums. Go crazy!

**Fergus Falls**

Friends almost everywhere you look,
everywhere you go, everywhere you
run or walk. Tall friends, short friends,
gentle friends, new friends, old friends,
unusually generous friends who will
stop what they're doing to help you.

Friends almost everywhere you look.
A friend to play games or sports with.
Lots of friends who you know your whole
life. Friends are almost everywhere here.
Smile if you see a good friend!

## Otter Tail County + Otter Tail County[2]

One thing I can
tell you for sure:
this is your home —
each of you can
read this and agree.

Tell us how this is
an amazing place.
Is it because you know
lots of wonderful things?

Can you tell us
one wonderful fact?
Use your imagination.
Nothing is too big or small.
Tell us something
you think no one else knows.

+

Over and over, I'll try to
think of something to cut
through clutter of thought.
Every single poem I write
reaches farther and farther.

This is to say that, yes, it
amazes how in Minnesota
I can feel super creative. I
love it here. It's almost fall.

Can you too feel the magic
of this home? I want you to
understand that each of you
nameless readers — children,
teenagers, adults — have got
your own exceptional ability.

## Bigfork, Minnesota + Itasca County

Breathe the air here.
It's sweet, isn't it. And isn't it easy
going across town since nothing is too
far, and you might see friends
on the way. Who appreciates
rivers? Who loves to fish? Who
keeps on the lookout for birds?

Maybe you were born here.
If so, raise your right hand.
Now I wonder who has been to
North Dakota. Or Michigan. Or
even New York City. Who's been to
South Dakota, Wyoming, Utah, Idaho,
or Oregon? And who has ever gone
to Alaska? No matter! All of you here
are lucky to live in this place of true beauty.

+

Imagine the perfect place.
This may be it—trees
and lakes and hills.
So many wonderful people
coming together so happy
and smart to live here.

Cold sometimes? Sure,
on occasion. Summers
up this way often bring crowds.
No, we don't mind sharing
this beautiful, magnificent land.
Yes, to our fine northern life.

## Trapper Creek Elementary

This is to tell you, my friends, to finish
reading one book, then start reading
another. That's how you learn.
Pretty soon, you'll read even more.
Pretty soon, you'll learn more.
Each book is a lesson. That's
reading. Some are easy. Some

can be harder, but the more you
read, the easier it gets.
Each book is different. I love
exciting books that help me
know new and wonderful things.

Eagles? I can find them in a book.
Lyrics to a song? I can find them in a book.
Earning a living as a doctor? That's in a book.
Making a sled? That's in a book.
Extra-fun games? I can find them in a book.
Nothing to do? I can read a story
that takes me to outer space, or to
a faraway island, or lets me travel back in time.
Reading can take you into the future too.
You can go anywhere if you know how to read.

**Talkeetna Elementary**

Try, my young friends, to not move
a single muscle. And don't talk.
Let yourself relax. Yes!
Keep breathing,
each breath deeper.
Every breath so deep.
Try not to move a muscle.
No, don't talk, not
a word, or sound. Be like a statue.

Everybody is different.
Lots of faces.
Everybody is different.
Maybe you're tall. Maybe short.
Everybody is different.
No two people are exactly alike—even
twins are different. Try not to move
a single muscle. Don't talk. Yes
relax, my young friends. Now,
yes, you can twist and talk. Maybe you'll sing!

## Kelly Elementary + Lewisburg[2]

Knowing how to be a good friend is
easier than you think. So is using
libraries. So is knowing how to
learn math, and to spell those words
you use often. If you come here

every day and try your best, you can
learn anything. Listen closely! Watch!
Each of us here have special talents.
Maybe you're better in music or sports.
Each of us here have so much to learn.
Nothing should stop us once we walk
through these school doors. Be
a helpful friend and good student.
Read another book! (Use the library!)
Yes, you're here today among friends.

+

Let's think of a town of kids small and tall,
exactly like the kids here. Is this the place?
Who has lived here their entire life? How
is it to live here? Is it anything like Hawaii?
Some of you have been to New York. Yes?
But now I wonder who likes a hot, hot tub.
Unless I'm mistaken, I think some of you
rejoice in playing outdoors in any weather.
Give yourselves a hand. You all are so big!

## Linntown Intermediate

Listen to your parents even
if you're tired. Listen close.
Notice how they're trying to help.
Notice how your teachers are also
trying to help as they look
over your schoolwork.
What's important to know?
No one is perfect. But here's a lesson —

if you don't quit, you'll find that
nothing is impossible. I'm here to say
the trick to never giving up is having fun,
even when progress is slow. I can
remember when I first played
music. It was new. I was bad, and most
every day was hard. But I continued,
doing what I'm telling you to do.
It's step by step. Get out of bed
and then get dressed. Then get ready.
Then school. How to have fun?
Enjoy friends! Practice something new!

## Seabury School[2]

Silliness is good for laughs.
Everyone likes a funny joke
and tall tale here in Tacoma.
But what if a black bear cub
undresses five feet from you.
Really! A naked black bear!
Yes, so close too! And silly!

Silly, so hugely silly! That's
crazy too, isn't it? Or magic,
how a bear can make a wish—
off goes black underwear so
only it is baby bear hair. Go
look at a bare bear. See it all!

## Clinton Public + Clinton Public[2]

Come read this
little skinny poem.
I love to
notice all sorts of
things everywhere.
One thing is you can
notice things too.

Please listen.
Understand you can
be someone who
looks more closely.
I promise that you
can then write poems.

+

Classes here include music.
Lots of kids sing really well
if they ever practice. Since I
never practiced, I had no fun
trying to sing. I was bad at it.
One day I practiced. Yes, so
now I can sing and have fun.

Perhaps you'll find this tip
useful. Yes, it's just for you.
Be brave. Don't quit. Climb.
Listen. Practice. Yes, you'll
improve if you want. Yes, I
can prove music is not magic.

## Denti[2] + Gansevoort

Don't be confused or afraid
Every poem is not a riddle.
No, poems are a lot of fun
to read, write or study. Just
imagine playing, you and I.

+

Get up, go to school,
act smart, learn
new things, take tests,
sit still, recess, friends,
eat lunch, sit
very still, lean
over sometimes,
obey your teacher,
read another book,
take the bus home.

# IV

## Monroe Central[2]

My riddle: the land where I'm from.
On top of the world, on the way to
North Pole. It's far away. You can
read about it in books. Yes, it's far—
on top of the world, on the way to
eagles, polar bears, wolves. People


can't believe a place full of magic,
everything so huge. Such wildlife.
No one can see it all. It's much fun
to hike, to climb mountains, to eat
reindeer sausage. Yes, it's very far.
A state like no other. Not Indiana.
Let's see if you know. Can you tell?

## Bloomington

Be a reader, my friends. Never
leave home without a book to
open whenever you're bored.
One book can change your life.
Maybe it's science fiction. Maybe
it's poetry. But remember this.
Never leave home without a book.
Good things happen when you read.
This poem is proof. If you can
open your mind, you might see, yes,
now you, too, can be a writer of books.

## Caston² + Caston²

Clear your minds. Listen to music
as you go about your fine Indiana
school day. Listen to these poems
that are surely most definitely not
ones you know & may lead you to
never being the same person again.

+

Cool kids, kids who love music,
art, math, and beautiful Indiana,
smart kids, super-duper-silly kids,
tricky kids, tall kids, very bright
ones, and very hungry ones who
need to eat lunch very very soon.

## Thompson[2] + OJ Neighbours[2]

The library is a favorite place. It
has as many books as you'd wish.
Only you can't read every one. So
many books. Books you can dream.
Picture books. Books you can't keep.
Short books, long books, big books.
Oh, there are DVDs to borrow too.
New magazines to read. It's so fun.

+

Okay, a poem that includes jello,
jelly, jam, smart kids who drink oj,

nice kids, naughty kids, nine or ten
easy math problems, a happy time
in the library, a big tray of spaghetti,
grins, groans, frowns, girls running,
hopping, skipping, all in a big rush,
boys in line to eat corn off the cob
or pizza, the teachers asking kids to
understand how to better learn. You
read this poem tonight with the writer
so you can have more fun with words.

## Lincoln + Lincoln²

Lots of poems rhyme, but
I write different kinds. I'll
notice everything going on. I
can write about math, science,
obnoxious bullies. I can
look around, see serious kids,
noisy kids, amazingly smart kids.

+

Let me explain the usual.
I write unusual poems. I
note what I can with pen.
Can you do this magic?
Of course. It's easy to
let your mind fully sail.
Note everything you can.

## Manchester Intermediate[2]

Maybe I'll remind you where I'm from.
Alaska, my friends, is surely not Indiana.
North Pole is Alaska's Santa Claus town,
colder than Fort Wayne. Alaska is magic.
Heroic sled dog teams that you can watch
every March at the famous Iditarod Race.
Summers may be short, but have long days
that kids love. They really really love it.
Every night is light. The kids stay up late,
really really late. It's the very best summer.

I started living in Alaska back in 1985. I
no longer am up there all the time. In
the school year months I often go visit
elementaries—kindergarten to 5$^{th}$ grade—
reaching many many students. So far
most kids enjoy the lessons even if I'm
elsewhere the next day. My job and life
demand always going around and around.
I drive, stop, unpack, play, pack, leave. I
am always so very happy to share Alaska
tales wherever I go. My friends, this is it.
Enjoy the rest of your time with me here.

## Ocean County + Ocean County[2]

One thing every one of us
can try to do is to make
every day better. Who has
an idea how to do that?
Nice clothes? Fun games?

Candy? Bananas, apples,
oranges, grapes? How about
using your beautiful brains?
New books from the library?
Try coming up with an idea
yourself. Name a favorite thing.

+

On summer days we might go
camping or go listen to music.
Everyone of us has a favorite
activity. This minute I have a
new thought that's a question:

Cats or dogs? It's quite basic.
Or maybe you prefer fish. To
understand any creature, you
need to observe close both in
the morning and also at night.
Yes, who's ever seen a firefly?

**Silver Bay Elementary**

Sometimes it's good to be
inside. You can play
lots of board games and watch
very good movies. You can
eat cupcakes, maybe while
reading excellent library books.

Being outside is good too.
A big field is great for sports.
You can climb huge trees,

even race up long hills.
Lot of bike trails to ride too,
even run two or three miles.
Maybe you'd rather swim
every day, perhaps at the beach.
Nature is everywhere.
There might be seagulls, deer,
a smelly skunk, a wild turkey,
raccoons. Pay attention!
You never know what you'll find.

**Bayville Elementary**

Be a reader, a friend,
an athlete, a leader, a listener.
You can be anything! Be
very brave, very strong, very
intelligent. Learn every
lesson. Learn to be kinder.
Learn to be more helpful. Learn
easy lessons and hard ones.

Every day there's more to learn.
Lessons in patience. Lessons in speed.
Every day, yes, there's more to learn.
Maybe you're tired. Take a nap!
Every day there's a different lesson —
no two days are ever the same.
Try something new. Keep practicing
and you will improve your talents.
Read another book. Then another.
You will never stop learning.

## Ocean Gate Elementary

Open your minds, my creative friends. Think
colors: blue, green, red, yellow, orange.
Everything, all of the colors like
a most fantastic rainbow. There's
nothing more amazing. Purples, like

grape juice. Browns, like dirt.
A white so bright, like the sun.
There are so many color shades—
early morning blue, midnight blue, blue-

eye blue, blue-jean blue, blueberry blue,
lake blue, bright electric blue, chalky blue,
easy blue, hard blue, ice-cold blue.
Maybe you can do the same with orange.
Energetic orange like fire. Or else
nice orange carrots. Or a cute little tangerine.
They're all different. There are also greens
and yellows and reds. Open your gigantic,
really colorful minds, my creative friends.
You all have beautiful rainbows within.

## Syracuse[2] + Fifth Street

Shy? Are any of you shy, my friends?
Yes? And what does it mean to be shy,
really, truly shy? Who here's a reader,
a happy and quite eager reader? Aha,
curious friends. Books are like magic.
Understand they can often help you
see our strange world in new ways.
Enter a book shyly. Read. Be brave.

+

For this poem, my friends,
I'll tell you a very short story.
From Alaska I come here
to tell you about moose, bear,
high mountains (the highest you'll

see in the United States). I come
to tell you that kids in Alaska
read lots of books, just like you.
Every day kids go to the library.
Every night they read. They're happy
to learn new things, just like you.

**Transitions**

Tell me if May is a favorite month.
Rain maybe. Warmer nights. Green trees
and colorful flowers. Baseball, softball,
no school during the long summer days.
Some of you may go on vacations
if you're lucky. Some of you may
try and learn something new here
in your hometown. Some of you may
open books and read of things you
never before imagined or thought possible.
School will be different next year.

# V

**Methow Valley Elementary**

Make a wish, then another.
Easy, my friends, to imagine
the most amazing things.
How about owning horses,
or your own boat, or maybe
winning a big championship.

Video games are great too,
and so is every sport.
Lots of fun things to wish for.
Long summer days with friends.
Endless hikes in the nearby wild.
You want to wish for what you love.

Every day, another new wish or dream.
Let yourself dream of amazing things
even if you're in a very bad
mood. Let yourself dream
even if you don't think you're a dreamer.
Never stop wishing or dreaming.
That's the best advice I have,
and I follow it myself. I wish to be
rid of troubles. I wish for the best
year ever. You, what do you wish for?

**East Omak Elementary**

Every day can be
an adventure, especially
summer. Long days mean
time to explore. Wide

open evenings—no homework!
Maybe ride a bike until late
and sleep at a friend's.
Know you may go camping.

Every day can fill with
lessons, especially summer.
Easy maybe to ride horses,
maybe to swim in lakes, maybe
eat fish that you catch.
Night comes and you sleep.
Then it's morning again,
another adventure ahead.
Reading is an adventure too.
You can dream with books!

## Sammamish + Sammamish²

Sometimes a poem can be
about lunch, or recess, or
maybe a wolf, dinosaur, or
monkey. A poem can be
about clouds, oceans,
mountains, or planets.
I mean a poem can be
silly or smart, can be
happy or sad. Or about you.

+

Silly me. Silly boys
and girls. Silly pizza.
Me, I'm hungry. I'm
making you a poem
and will eat this in a
minute. Silly me. I'm
in a silly silly mood. I
surely am hungry. Yes!
Have a silly sandwich!

**Green Hill + Northeast**

Go to the library. Go
read a book. Go in line to
eat lunch. Go eat
everything on your tray. Go
now. Go quickly. Go

however you must. Go
in the next minute. Go
like you really mean it.
Let me say it again: Go.

+

No is a good word. No!
Over and over we say it. No
running. No kicking. No
tickling. No screaming. No
hurrying. No worrying. No
eating with your mouth open. No
accidents. No fighting. No
spitting. No bullying. No
throwing food. No! No! No!

### Cochise County + Cochise County[2]

Cowboys here? Yes,
of course. Beautiful
cowgirls also live
here. Come visit
if you truly love
summer heat,
easy winter,

cool spring nights, wind.
Of course, please
understand that
no one knows
this high desert like
you all do.

+

Can you tell me that the music
of the desert is wind? Yes? No?
Can you tell me about magic?
How do we live on this earth?
I'd say some people love to ski.
Some people love their horses.
Everybody loves their favorite

cat or dog, their favorite music.
Or else some people love to go
up in balloons. What about you?
No one I know doesn't like fun.
Tell me about fun. Trick or treat?
Your best friend? Some candy?

## Enterprise Elementary School

Examine this poem. It contains what is
next to you and what is across from you.
There are friends and outlaws
(each might be the same here).
Read this poem very carefully
please. Or read it very quickly.
Read it and realize how
it's a little bit different.
See if you can find the truth.
Every one of you can read it.

Examine this poem. It has what you
like and dislike. It has
everything and nothing, just like life.
Maybe it has hunger. Maybe money.
Eggs too. And a hamburger with fries.
No, don't try to eat this poem
(the paper will not taste very good).
Are you tired of this poem yet?
Read some more since it's not over.
You might see how it's about you.

See how there's real beauty here.
Cold days still, but it's getting warmer.
How do we know all this? Look
outside. There you might find eagles
or bears. Here inside this poem, you'll find
lots to think about. It's like a mirror.

**Seven Locks**[2]

Start your day with breakfast. Who eats
eggs in the morning? Scrambled eggs are
very tasty with toast. Don't watch the tv.
Eat your eggs slowly and quietly. Smile
next time you eat eggs. Make that a plan.

Lots of children would rather eat cereal,
or pancakes, or waffles. Alaska and Ohio
children, too. How they eat is not magic.
Know that they sit down with clean fork.
spoon, and knife. They also use napkins.

## Houston Clear Lake

How to best listen to music?
One day pick up an instrument
(unless you're already holding one).
Saxophone, guitar, violin, banjo,
trumpet. What matters is
opening yourself and playing one
note, then another. That's how you're

certain to learn. Do you
love to explore? Here's what I know:
everyone can play. Drums, piano,
accordion, bass. Cello, harmonica, flute.
Rock and roll. Classical. Folk. Jazz.

Listen close. Stay open. Look long enough—
an instrument will come to you.
Keep practicing—and you will go places,
even farther than you ever imagined.

## Athens Autumn Harvest Moon Fest + Woodford[2]

A special poem here that will
take you, my friends, past summer
heat to the end of September.
Each day we're thankful. No longer hot.
Not yet cold (perhaps a light frost
some mornings if we're up early).

A special poem here that will help you
understand, my friends, that this is
the season for apple, pumpkin, watermelon,
unless you prefer your vegetables —
mustard greens, broccoli, spinach, potato.
Never have you seen such long, beautiful,

happy carrots, such perfect ears of corn,
and we want to know about zucchini,
radish, pepper, and parsnip. It's all so
very tempting. All you have to do next is
enjoy going home to cook. Did I
say kale? How about cabbage? Now I'm
thinking soup, and salad,

maybe leafy lettuce with cucumbers.
Or a great big pot of gumbo with
okra and onion that will warm you.
Never have we had so much good fresh

food to chop and throw in a pot or bowl.
Every meal is an adventure. Even
small gardens can offer you so much
tomato and collards. If you're lucky, cauliflower.

+

What to do? Who to see? How
often to eat? Where best to go
order a slushy or smoothie to
drink? You can find new good
friends here. You can buy stuff
of course—books, t-shirts, also
rings for an ear, a toe, a finger.
Do what makes you very glad.

## St. Paul Elementary

Some of you are feeling happy
today. Who? Some of you love

playing games. Who? Some of you
are hungry, tired, sad, or thinking
up ideas. Who? Some of you
like to eat extra-cheesy pizza. Who?

Each of us have favorite sweets—
lollipops, brownies, ice cream. What?
Each of us have a favorite color—
maybe red, green, yellow, blue. What?
Each of us have favorite animals—
naughty puppies, kittens, even hamsters.
This is a poem that has questions
and answers. Who here loves
reading? Who here is reading books
yesterday, today, and tomorrow?

## Littleton Academy

Littler kids and bigger kids
in every classroom. Some
talk more than others. Some
talk less. Some always have
lots of books. Some have less.
Every student has their own
talent. Some are better with animals
or plants. Some are better at math.
No one has no talent. Maybe you play

a music instrument or a sport. Maybe you
can teach your parents or grandparents
about computers. Maybe you
do chores for an elderly neighbor.
Every student has their own talent.
Maybe you're a reader. Maybe
you're a leader. Maybe you're a friend.

## Allen County[2] + Allen County Intermediate

Are you happier or sadder now? Are you a
left-hander or right-hander? Can you yell
loud in an emergency? Can you even spell
*emergency*? Do you like it odd or strange
now and again? Do you like having fun?

Can I tell you a fun thing about music?
Oh, it's not all that difficult to learn to
use a fiddle, banjo, guitar, piano. You
need to learn whatever seems like fun.
This poem says to have fun. Don't quit.
You can learn to make work into play.

+

Ants are little. Aunts are big.
Let me tell you what you already know.
Lots of words are funny and strange.
Eye is an eye. But I see you.
No means no. But you know about yes.

Claws is not clause (nor Santa Claus). Two is not too
or to. Where is not wear. And hair is not hare
(unless you have a rabbit with a beard).
No, why is not Y. Nor is a pear a pair.
Tails are not tales, though
you can tell a story about a dog wagging

its own happy rear end. Wait! What's your weight?
No, wait is not weight and here is not hear.
To tell the truth, there is not their, or
even they're. C is not sea. See?
Rite is not write. Am I right? Reed is not read.
Maybe you also once read about red.
Ewe? Is that you? Or is that someone new? Or is it a gnu?
Dew? Do you know what makes dew? Do you?
I'm this busy bee with words. Can you be a bee?
Are you more like a B or an R? Who ate eight cookies?
Ten cookies? Who ate four for breakfast?
Even one wee piece of cookie means we won. Peace.

**Illuminations**

If you want to write a poem,
let me say, yes, my friends,
let's do just that. We will fire
up our brains, and have
much fun. I tell you, my friends,
if you want to write a poem,
nothing can stop you.
A poem you write might include
Things you love the most.
It might include dogs, cats,
or horses. It might include
new toys, old dolls, or ice cream.
Some might include your mom or dad.

## Alton[2]

A man from Alaska
loves to visit and tell
tricky little poems. It
opens young minds to
new kinds of real fun.

# Coda

## My Poem is Here

Make a poem here! Have
yourself some real fun, like

playing a game, but with words.
One thing I try to do with
every poem is keeping it simple.
Many of my poems have

ideas I've been thinking about.
Simple ideas and simple words!

How can you write one?
Easily, I think, after
reading this book. On the next page,
end this book with your own poem.

**MY POEM IS HERE**

M
Y

P
O
E
M

I
S

H
E
R
E

(Send your original MY POEM IS HERE acrostic to Ken Waldman by postal mail to 3705 Arctic #1551, Anchorage AK 99503 or by email to ken@kenwaldman.com and you might find your poem in a book some day — after reading this book you will have ideas how to do this!)

# A Page For You To Write or Draw Whatever You Want!

(Maybe you'll even draw a self-portrait to go along with your poem -- turn the page and see how Ken Waldman drew himself on the very last page of the book.)

## BIO

**Ken Waldman** has drawn on 40 years as an Alaska resident to produce poems, stories, and fiddle tunes that combine into a performance uniquely his. 12 CDs mix Appalachian-style string-band music with original poetry. 24 books include 17 full-length poetry collections, a memoir, 3 children's poetry books, a creative writing manual, a novel, and a short story collection. Since 1995 he's toured full-time, performing at leading festivals, concert series, arts centers, and clubs, including the Kennedy Center Millennium Stage, Dodge Poetry Festival, and Woodford Folk Festival (Queensland, Australia). He's also visited more than 250 schools in 35 states as well as over 100 colleges and universities. For more about Ken Waldman, www.kenwaldman.com and www.trumpsonnets.com. And for more about Ridgeway Press, www.ridgewaypress.org.

**And a last word from Ken Waldman:**

Having worked with young writers for over thirty years, when teaching poetry I mostly stay away from rhyme, which so often can feel forced, and instead model either repetition, which offers easy rhythm, or acrostics, which offers playfulness (and free verse flexibility). Advanced writers can be especially challenged when trying their own double acrostics, which are noted in this book by the ² in the titles (which signify both the first letters and last letters of the line are an acrostic). Basic writers can succeed by writing more rudimentary acrostics. So, a last rudimentary sample (and lesson):

All
Can
Realize
Original
Singular
Thoughts
In
Creating
Simply